Improvement Le

LEAN SIX SIGM
TOLLGATES AND (

This is a comprehensive, yet extremely simple to use guide for all Lean Six Sigma project team leaders and Master Black Belts. It provides readers with the questions they should be asking at key stages of a business improvement project, and the the key components of work that should be considered before moving on to each progressive phase of a project.

by George Lee Sye

MAJOR TOPICS

The DMAIC Philosophy - 20 Step DMAIC Roadmap - Project Tollgates (Lean and Six Sigma) - Project Checklists (Lean and Six Sigma)

SOARENT PUBLISHING
PO Box 267, Ravenshoe, Qld, AUSTRALIA, 4888

Other books by the author - https://georgeleesye.com/

This book is produced as part of a body of knowledge for business improvement practitioners - https://www.9skillsfactory.com/ processmasterywithleansixsigma

CONTENTS

Introduction 4

    Book Layout 5

Chapter 1 - Lean and Six Sigma Projects.............................7

    The DMAIC Philosophy...7

    DMAIC Overview 9

    A 20 Step DMAIC Roadmap...11

Chapter 2 - Project Tollgates 18

    DEFINE Phase Tollgate Questions....................................18

    MEASURE Phase Tollgate Questions.................................21

    ANALYSE Phase Tollgate Questions.................................24

    IMPROVE Phase Tollgate Questions 27

    CONTROL Phase Tollgate Questions 31

Chapter 3 - Project Checklists 34

    Project CHARTER Checklist 34

    DEFINE Phase Checklist 36

    MEASURE Phase Checklist...38

    ANALYSE Phase Checklist 40

    IMPROVE Phase Checklist...42

    CONTROL Phase Checklist...46

Wrap Up..48

About the Author 49

Introduction

When I wrote my original Lean Six Sigma textbook - Process Mastery with Lean Six Sigma, I did it because of my dissatisfaction with the extent of information that was available in text form. It seemed to me that the information I had access to was incomplete, no single text provided the depth of information I desired while learning to be a competent Black Belt.

If that was how I felt, then I was sure other people felt that way also.

Surprise surprise .... the book was a hit and sold out.

Why has it been so popular, what is it about the book that continues to draw practitioners around the world to own a copy?

One of the elements of the book that we receive great feedback about has been the tollgates and checklists that are provided after each of the DMAIC phases. They are comprehensive guides that can be used by Green Belts, Black Belts and even Master Black Belts who are engaged in mentoring roles in their organisations.

What made this element work so well was the fact that we actually wrote the questions out for practitioners to ask themselves or ask of others.

Well the good news is this ... all of those have been reproduced here for your use.

Book Layout

For ease of reference, I have presented the book in a three-part format.

Part 1 - The DMAIC Model

The first part of the book presents a standard 20-step DMAIC roadmap that sits behind the application of both Lean and Six Sigma methodologies. The entire 20 steps are not presented in a single diagram as this format of publishing makes it difficult to produce the diagram in such a way that you can read it.

What I have done is broken the 20 steps into 5 separate diagrams, each one representing one of the DMAIC phases. If you would like a copy of the entire roadmap, you are provided a link to our website where you can download a printable pdf file.

I should point that this roadmap was never meant to be *the* roadmap.

It is however, a pretty useful model for practitioners of both Lean and Six Sigma in a project context. I'm sure you'll find that few models provide such a simple and flexible approach.

I have referenced this roadmap when identifying where each of the tollgates is undertaken.

Part 2 - Tollgates

Part 2 presents the actual tollgate questions.

These can be used for self review or as a basis for a Master Black Belt to conduct a tollgate review for a project being led by a Green Belt or Black Belt.

I know you'll find these *extremely* useful.

Part 3 - Checklists

Part 3 provides you with checklists for each of the phases of DMAIC. These are used by the project team leader to make sure they are doing (or at least considering) the right pieces of work as they move through an improvement project.

They have application to both Lean and Six Sigma projects.

Well, no use procrastinating, let's get straight into it.

Enjoy.

Chapter 1 - Lean and Six Sigma Projects

The DMAIC Philosophy

To successfully employ the DMAIC approach, a Black Belt must be familiar with more than just the tools of process improvement. They must be familiar with the steps to take within each of the 'phases' of the Lean Six Sigma process improvement methodology.

Before discussing a 'roadmap', let me discuss the philosophy behind my approach to Lean Six Sigma. This philosophy is based on two things:

> (a) My experience and observations of projects that have generated returns totalling 100s of millions of dollars; and

> (b) The belief that the only constant in process improvement work is the start and end point – there are many ways to get to the desired outcome.

Philosophy

1. There is no one-way to do Lean or Six Sigma.

There are many effective ways to get from the start point to the desired end point. Much like a traveller finding her way to a new destination, the Black Belt is able to design his or her path through the steps of DMAIC according to their particular circumstances.

2. There are some elements that must be completed for every project.

These include:

    (a) define the PROBLEM up front,

    (b) collect reliable DATA with relevant stratification variables,

    (c) find the SOURCES of most variation,

    (d) find and validate ROOT CAUSES of that variation,

    (e) generate and select SOLUTIONS that treat root causes and fit criteria important to the customer and the business,

    (f) IMPLEMENT solutions using project management skills,

    (g) STANDARDISE the process and CONTROL its performance, and finally,

    (h) CELEBRATE at the end of the project.

3. Whilst appearing linear, any 'roadmap' is iterative in that it is often necessary to go back at some point or move forward at other points in the process.

There will be occasions when easy wins or 'just do it' solutions are implemented while the analysis phase continues, in effect working in two parts of the DMAIC process at the one time.

The only constant across Lean Six Sigma projects is the start and end point. The project starts with the identification of a performance gap, and the final destination is the closing of that gap. There is no one path between the two points.

4. Black Belts are given an extensive toolbox, but not every tool needs to be used.

Much like a motor mechanic working on different cars, they draw tools from that toolbox when they are needed for a specific purpose. Each tool helps generate answers to specific questions, and when the questions arise, that is the time for the tool or tools to be used.

5. Special cause variation must be eliminated before working on common cause variation.

A process with special cause variation is unstable. This 'out of control' situation must be resolved and the process stabilised before the full power of Lean Six Sigma can be utilised.

So ..... when using this roadmap, or any other, I would suggest keeping in mind that it is a starting point on your journey to mastering Lean Six Sigma. Over time you will find yourself creating your own general guidelines.

Be cautious to ensure that any roadmap does not become prescriptive and kills the innovation and adaptability of your Lean Six Sigma work.

DMAIC Overview

The following is a simple overview of the key generic activities of a Lean Six Sigma project. Not all of these activities apply to all projects.

Suffice to say they simply give us an understanding of what is commonly involved.

Define Phase

- Identify the improvement opportunity

- Allocate the project to a team leader

- Develop the project charter (an activity that involves the participation of team leader, process owner and project champion)

- Start up the project team

- Document the key elements of the process being worked on

Measure Phase

- Plan the collection of data

- Validate the measurement system used to collect data

- Collect the data

- Measure baseline performance (process capability or process efficiency)

Analyse Phase

- Evaluate process stability

- Eliminate special cause variation if it exists OR go straight on to identifying the source of variation or waste

- Analyse cause & effect relationships where you need to

Improve Phase

- Generate and select solutions

- Mitigate potential errors or consequences

- Develop the implementation plan

- Implement solutions

Control Phase

- Standardise processes

- Develop monitoring and response plans

- Monitor performance

- Respond to deviations from plan

A 20 Step DMAIC Roadmap

The 20-step process shown in the roadmap on the following page has proven successful in guiding thousands of Black Belts and Green Belts in the effective employment of the DMAIC approach.

It may prove useful in helping *you* begin your journey to mastery of Lean Six Sigma through improvement project work.

Tollgates / Stakeholder Check-ins

While each company might develop its own approach to these components, tollgates and stakeholder check-ins are vital to (a) the learning process and (b) engaging people impacted by any change resulting from the project work.

These points are identified in diagrammatic form on the DMAIC roadmap.

Define Phase Steps

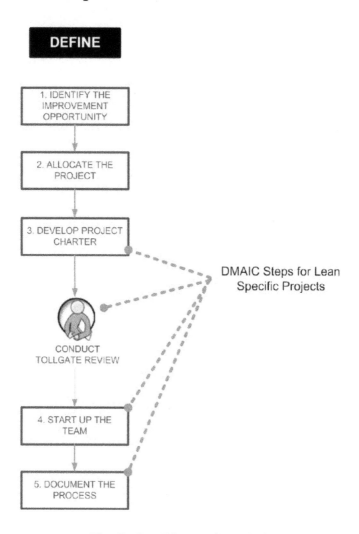

The Define Phase of DMAIC

Measure Phase Steps

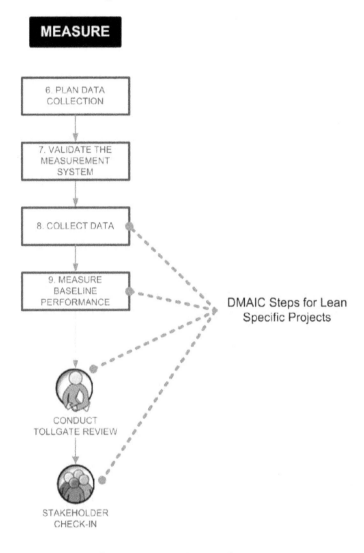

The Measure Phase of DMAIC

Analyse Phase Steps

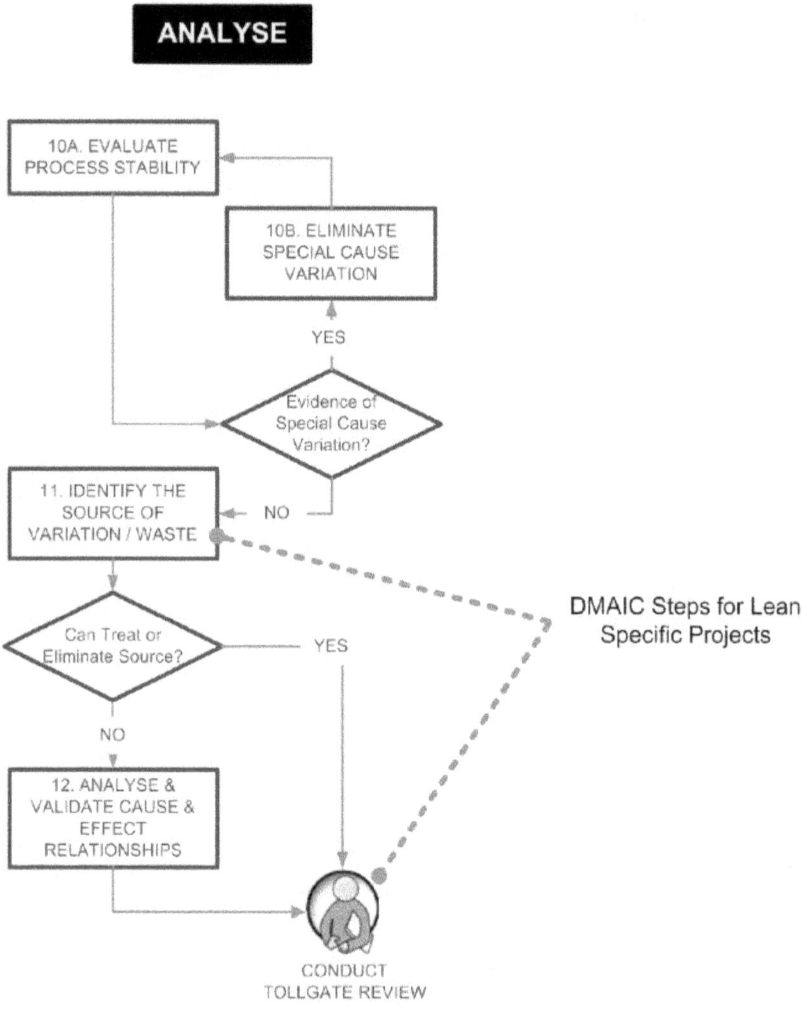

The Analyse Phase of DMAIC

Improve Phase Steps

IMPROVE

13. GENERATE AND SELECT SOLUTIONS

14. MITIGATE POTENTIAL ERRORS / CONSEQUENCES

15. DEVELOP IMPLEMENTATION PLAN

CONDUCT TOLLGATE REVIEW

STAKEHOLDER CHECK-IN

16. IMPLEMENT SOLUTIONS

DMAIC Steps for Lean Specific Projects

The Improve Phase of DMAIC

Control Phase Steps

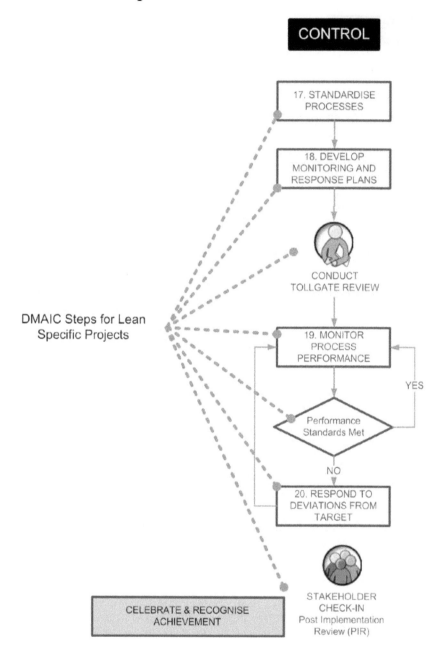

The Control Phase of DMAIC

If you would like to download a copy of the 20 Step Roadmap in its entirety, visit the website here - https://www.9skillsfactory.com/ - and check the FREE downloads pages.

Chapter 2 - Project Tollgates

A tollgate review is effectively a process for ensuring this:

- The project is progressing,

- It will continue to progress,

- It is going to add value to the organisation, and

- The Black Belt (or Green Belt) is effectively employing the tools and processes of the continual improvement methodology being used, in this case Lean and Six Sigma.

DEFINE Phase Tollgate Questions

One of the key skills of any manager or leader is the art of questioning. Good questions promote thought, focus and learning. The following questions are the kind that may be asked by your Master Black Belt or Lean Six Sigma Project Champion during a 'Define Phase Tollgate Review'.

This tollgate takes place between step 3 and step 4 on our 20-step roadmap.

The Charter (Lean and Six Sigma Projects)

What is the problem / opportunity?

Why is this project worth doing?

How do you know that?

What is the scope of this project?

How did you decide that was the scope?

What key business performance measures will be affected by this project?

How will it affect those measures?

How will you know if this project is successful?

Has a similar project been undertaken elsewhere?

How can we learn from that work?

What are your project milestones?

What communications have you planned to undertake with key stakeholders?

The Team (Lean and Six Sigma Projects)

Who is on the team?

How and why did you select those members?

What level of commitment do you expect to get from your team?

How do you propose to deal with that? (if relevant)

What agreements have you established with your project champion and process owner for how you will work together?

What level of commitment do you expect to get from the process owner?

How do you propose to deal with that? (if relevant)

Customer Participation (Six Sigma Projects Only)

Who are the customers of the process?

What involvement have you planned for customers?

General (Lean and Six Sigma Projects)

What challenges do you anticipate you will have with this project?

What risks could affect project progress?

How are you going to deal with those risks?

What is your plan from here?

How can I assist?

MEASURE Phase Tollgate Questions

The following questions are the kind that may be asked by your Master Black Belt or Lean Six Sigma Project Champion during a 'Measure Phase Tollgate Review'.

This tollgate takes place between step 9 and step 10 on our 20-step roadmap.

Charter / Scope (Lean and Six Sigma Projects)

What revisions need to be or have been made to the charter?

How has the scope of the project changed?

What changes need to be made to the project time line?

Process Documentation (Lean and Six Sigma Projects)

How did you document the process?

Who was involved?

How do you know this is the actual process used today?

Data Collection (Six Sigma Projects Only)

What variables did you collect data on?

How did you choose those variables?

How did you collect the data?

How do you know the data is valid and reliable?

How do you / will you know the system for measuring performance is reliable and not affecting the result?

How much data did you collect?

How did you choose your sample size?

How do you know it is a representative sample?

What time period is covered by the data you collected?

How do you know that time period is not too long or too short to be valid?

Baseline Performance / Capability (Six Sigma Projects Only)

Did you analyse process capability?

What were the results?

Did you calculate a baseline process sigma?

What is the baseline process sigma calculation for the process?

How did you define defects, a unit and opportunities?

Baseline Performance / Efficiency (Lean Projects Only)

Did you analyse process cycle efficiency?

What were the results?

How do you know the cycle time data you used is valid and reliable?

The Team (Lean and Six Sigma Projects)

Who has been involved as a team member to date?

What is the attendance rate of team members?

What level of commitment are you experiencing with your team?

What level of commitment do you perceive from the process owner?

What do you plan to do to positively impact the level of commitment demonstrated by [insert identity of key stakeholder]?

What does the team understand of the desired outcome?

What involvement have customers had with this project to date?

What involvement have you planned for customers?

Communications (Lean and Six Sigma Projects)

What communications have you planned to undertake with key stakeholders?

General (Lean and Six Sigma Projects)

What challenges are you experiencing that I can assist with?

What is your plan from here?

ANALYSE Phase Tollgate Questions

The following questions are the kind that may be asked by your Master Black Belt or Lean Six Sigma Project Champion during an 'Analyse Phase Tollgate Review'.

This tollgate takes place between step 12 and step 13 on our 20-step roadmap.

Charter / Scope (Lean and Six Sigma Projects)

What revisions need to be made to the charter?

How has the scope of the project changed?

What changes need to be made to the project time line?

Stability Analysis (Six Sigma Projects Only)

Did you observe any special cause variation in this process?

How do you propose to treat that variation?

After you treat it, what are your intentions?

Sources of Variation (Six Sigma Projects Only)

What key variables have you identified as sources of process variation?

How do you know these are sources of variation?

How did you validate these as sources of variation?

Are you able to eliminate these from the process?

What course of action are you going to undertake with these now?

Cause and Effect Analysis (Six Sigma Projects Only)

What major causes of variation (or problem) have you identified?

How did you go about identifying these as major causes?

Who was involved in the process?

How did you validate the cause and effect relationships?

Sources of Waste (Lean Projects Only)

Have you analysed the process from a waste perspective?

How did you do that?

What did your analysis reveal?

Where is the greatest opportunity to remove waste from the process?

How did you validate that?

Have you studied cycle time?

Where is most time consumed in this process?

How did you determine that?

How much time is spent adding value in this process?

How do you know that?

Which steps have you broken down further into sub-process flowcharts?

Why did you choose to break those steps down?

What opportunities exist to reduce the non-value adding or unnecessary time?

How have you validated that?

Communications (Lean and Six Sigma Projects)

What communications have you undertaken with key stakeholders?

General (Lean and Six Sigma Projects)

What challenges are you experiencing that I can assist with?

What is your plan from here?

IMPROVE Phase Tollgate Questions

The following questions are the kind that may be asked by your Master Black Belt or Lean Six Sigma Project Champion during a 'Improve Phase Tollgate Review'.

This tollgate takes place between steps 15 and 16 on our 20-step roadmap.

Charter / Scope (Lean and Six Sigma Projects)

What revisions need to be made to the charter?

How has the scope of the project changed?

What changes need to be made to the project time line?

Benchmarking (Six Sigma Projects Only)

Did you undertake any benchmarking studies?

What were they?

What was the basis for choosing these places for your benchmarking?

How was the benchmarking study undertaken?

What were the results?

How did these results impact your process improvement work?

Solution Identification (Lean and Six Sigma Projects)

What are your proposed solutions or changes?

What process did you use to identify these?

How did you make your final choice of solutions?

Who was involved in the process?

How do you know these solutions will make a difference?

How are these solutions linked to validated causes or key factors?

Process Improvement (Lean and Six Sigma Projects)

Do you intend changing the process (steps) itself?

What does the new process look like?

What principles did you apply in redesigning it?

Who was involved in the process?

How do you know this new process will result in an improved outcome?

What benefits will this new process offer?

Piloting (Lean and Six Sigma Projects)

Did you pilot any of these solutions?

Where did you do that pilot?

How did you choose that location?

How long did the pilot study take?

How did you go about measuring the success of the pilot?

What did you learn from the pilot?

Solution Implementation (Lean and Six Sigma Projects)

What is your plan for implementing these solutions?

Who was involved in the planning process?

What risks have you identified?

How have you planned to deal with these risks?

How will the implementation of these solutions affect other parts of the business?

Change Strategy (Lean and Six Sigma Projects)

What work have you undertaken to identify stakeholder commitment?

What is your plan for getting buy-in from key stakeholders?

How do you propose to engage those that may exhibit resistance?

What systems or structures require changing to support the proposed solutions or the new level of performance expected?

How do you know that your solutions will be sustainable over the long term?

Monitoring / Tracking Benefits (Lean and Six Sigma Projects)

How do you plan to monitor the performance of the process post implementation?

Given what you know now, what benefits do you expect to see from the project?

How do you propose to track these benefits?

General (Lean and Six Sigma Projects)

What challenges are you experiencing that I can assist with?

What is your plan from here?

CONTROL Phase Tollgate Questions

The following questions are the kind that may be asked by your Master Black Belt or Lean Six Sigma Project Champion during a 'Control Phase Tollgate Review'.

This tollgate takes place between step 18 and step 19 on our 20-step roadmap.

Charter / Scope (Lean and Six Sigma Projects)

What revisions need to be or have been made to the charter?

How has the scope of the project changed?

What changes need to be made to the project time line?

Process Standardisation (Lean and Six Sigma Projects)

Did your work result in changes to the process of work?

How did you document that new process?

How do you plan to institutionalise that new process?

Customer Impact (Lean and Six Sigma Projects)

How did you go about identifying customers' needs and requirements for this process?

How did you validate those customers' requirements?

How do you know changes in the process will not adversely affect customers?

Process Performance Monitoring & Control (Lean and Six Sigma Projects)

How do you intend to monitor process performance?

What specific variables have you included in your monitoring plan?

Why did you choose those variables over others not included?

Which of these are really lead indicators that provide early warning of changes to outcomes?

How will performance results be communicated?

What control mechanisms do you plan to put in place so operators can respond to deviations from the expected level of performance?

Benefits (Lean and Six Sigma Projects)

What improvements have you observed to date?

What benefits have been realised and captured?

How are benefits going to be tracked?

How do you intend to ensure that claimed benefits are real?

Learnings (Lean and Six Sigma Projects)

What have you learnt during this experience?

What learnings have you shared?

What learnings should be shared?

How do you intend to make your learnings accessible to other project team leaders?

How have you documented your project work?

How can people access information about your work?

Team Recognition (Lean and Six Sigma Projects)

What activities have you undertaken to date to recognise and reward team members for their work?

What have you planned to do to recognise and reward team members for their contribution?

Chapter 3 - Project Checklists

If you have responded appropriately to each of the following statements, then you are ready to move forward in the relevant phase of your project.

Project CHARTER Checklist

Lean and Six Sigma Projects

You can confirm that the project is important to undertake now by explaining the relationship between the project and business goals.

☐ Yes   ☐ No   ☐ NA

The leadership team of the business supports the project.

☐ Yes   ☐ No   ☐ NA

The project is a problem or opportunity that is based on an existing and repetitive business process. (Fits the DMAIC methodology)

☐ Yes   ☐ No   ☐ NA

Team membership and roles are defined.

☐ Yes   ☐ No   ☐ NA

Have agreed upon the definition of the problem in a clear statement of what is happening, how long it has been occurring and what its impact to the business is.

☐ Yes   ☐ No   ☐ NA

The primary metric has been defined, along with the baseline KPI.

☐ Yes   ☐ No   ☐ NA

A preliminary target KPI has been defined and agreed to by the team.

☐ Yes   ☐ No   ☐ NA

The improvement goal/s for the team have been agreed upon by team members and the project champion, and stated in measurable terms that are linked to the problem. No solutions are proposed in the goal statements.

☐ Yes   ☐ No   ☐ NA

Limitations or constraints that may impact project work or potential solution selection have been identified and discussed with the Champion and Sponsor.

☐ Yes   ☐ No   ☐ NA

The scope of the project is clearly defined to ensure focus.

☐ Yes   ☐ No   ☐ NA

The benefit type for this project has been defined.

☐ Yes   ☐ No   ☐ NA

Initial 'one off' and 'annualised' cost benefits have been estimated.

☐ Yes   ☐ No   ☐ NA

Performance to date over a relevant baseline period has been graphically represented and is available for presentation if required.

☐ Yes   ☐ No   ☐ NA

A preliminary plan or schedule for the project work is prepared.

☐ Yes   ☐ No   ☐ NA

DEFINE Phase Checklist

Lean and Six Sigma Projects

A project charter has been developed and agreed to by the Champion, Process Owner and Project Team Leader.

☐ Yes   ☐ No   ☐ NA

The schedule and associated deliverables for each phase of the project has been stated.

☐ Yes   ☐ No   ☐ NA

Operating agreements have been established with the Champion, the Process Owner, the Team, and the Master Black Belt (where applicable).

☐ Yes   ☐ No   ☐ NA

The team shares a common vision of where the project will take them and the desired outcome or goal is captured in words.

☐ Yes   ☐ No   ☐ NA

The team has identified the short and long term consequences of not doing the project work.

☐ Yes   ☐ No   ☐ NA

The team has identified the short and long term benefits of doing the project work.

☐ Yes   ☐ No   ☐ NA

The tangible products and / or services (the output of the process) are defined.

☐ Yes   ☐ No   ☐ NA

The material and data inputs to the process have been identified.

☐ Yes   ☐ No   ☐ NA

The resources that enable the process to turn inputs into outputs have been identified.

☐ Yes   ☐ No   ☐ NA

The process as it occurs today has been mapped using an Activity Flowchart.

☐ Yes   ☐ No   ☐ NA

All work has been summarised in the form of an IPO worksheet.

☐ Yes   ☐ No   ☐ NA

Project storyboard or poster has been commenced.

☐ Yes   ☐ No   ☐ NA

A strategy for communicating to key stakeholders and relevant parties has been agreed to by all team members.

☐ Yes   ☐ No   ☐ NA

Team members have developed an 'Elevator Speech' for the purpose of consistently communicating the key elements of the project.

☐ Yes   ☐ No   ☐ NA

MEASURE Phase Checklist

Six Sigma Project Specific

The measure or measures relevant to performance of concern have been identified.

☐ Yes   ☐ No   ☐ NA

Potential sources of variation (stratification variables) have been defined and captured on the data collection plan.

☐ Yes   ☐ No   ☐ NA

Each measure has been operationally defined to ensure consistency in the method of collection.

☐ Yes   ☐ No   ☐ NA

Operational definitions have been tested to ensure consistent interpretation.

☐ Yes   ☐ No   ☐ NA

A data collection plan has been prepared in which the most likely 'cause' variables have been identified.

☐ Yes   ☐ No   ☐ NA

Measurement system variation has been analysed to ensure that its contribution to total variation is acceptable, OR alternatively the team has confidence in the measurement system used to collect data and has made the decision not to study measurement system variation.

☐ Yes   ☐ No   ☐ NA

Sample sizes have been calculated to provide designated confidence levels for relevant statistics (mean and or proportions).

☐ Yes   ☐ No   ☐ NA

Data has been collected in such a way as to link stratification variables and likely cause variables to performance measures.

☐ Yes   ☐ No   ☐ NA

A baseline Process Sigma has been calculated.

☐ Yes   ☐ No   ☐ NA

The capability of the process to produce outputs within customer tolerances has been studied and Capability Index values have been calculated.

☐ Yes   ☐ No   ☐ NA

Lean Project Specific

Average cycle time data for each step of the process has been collected.

☐ Yes   ☐ No   ☐ NA

Value adding process steps (and corresponding time) have been identified.

☐ Yes   ☐ No   ☐ NA

Baseline Process Cycle Efficiency (PCE) has been calculated.

☐ Yes   ☐ No   ☐ NA

ANALYSE Phase Checklist

Six Sigma Project Specific

Analysed performance data using control charts and are able to state whether the process is or is not in a state of statistical control.

☐ Yes   ☐ No   ☐ NA

Stratified the data in multiple ways to find the source of variation and the appropriate level at which to analyse for root causes.

☐ Yes   ☐ No   ☐ NA

Validated the differences between potential sources of variation using statistical methods.

☐ Yes   ☐ No   ☐ NA

Conducted a root cause analysis and generated relevant root cause hypothesis to explain the effect being observed.

☐ Yes   ☐ No   ☐ NA

Validated root causes using appropriate evidentiary methods.

☐ Yes   ☐ No   ☐ NA

Commenced work to implement any 'early wins' identified by the team during the analysis phase.

☐ Yes   ☐ No   ☐ NA

Lean Project Specific

Conducted an analysis of process performance against Takt Time and have identified any constraints and time traps.

☐ Yes   ☐ No   ☐ NA

Identified where the greatest opportunity is to improve efficiency against the key project metric.

☐ Yes   ☐ No   ☐ NA

Visually examined the sub-process flowchart and identified bottlenecks, reworks, inefficient or unnecessary handoffs that may be contributing to the effect being observed.

☐ Yes   ☐ No   ☐ NA

Commenced work to implement any 'early wins' identified by the team during the analysis phase.

☐ Yes   ☐ No   ☐ NA

IMPROVE Phase Checklist

Six Sigma Specific Project

A benchmarking study of relevant organisations or work sites has been undertaken and adaptable ideas have been identified.

☐ Yes ☐ No ☐ NA

A wide range of potential solutions were identified with the involvement of key process participants / operators.

☐ Yes ☐ No ☐ NA

Final solutions that treat validated causes of variation have been chosen by the team using a systematic decision making process.

☐ Yes ☐ No ☐ NA

Unintended consequences of implementing proposed solutions have been identified and a plan created for dealing with these.

☐ Yes ☐ No ☐ NA

A risk management plan has been put in place to deal with risks that affect the achievement of implementation project objectives.

☐ Yes ☐ No ☐ NA

Have conducted a pilot study to identify what would occur under conditions of full-scale implementation.

☐ Yes ☐ No ☐ NA

Evaluated results of the pilot study and confirmed that project goals can be achieved.

☐ Yes ☐ No ☐ NA

Have modified the implementation plan as a result of the learnings from the pilot study.

☐ Yes   ☐ No   ☐ NA

A training plan for aligning skills to the requirements of the solution has been prepared.

☐ Yes   ☐ No   ☐ NA

Have developed a communications plan to support implementation.

☐ Yes   ☐ No   ☐ NA

Anticipated levels of commitment to proposed solutions have been analysed and stakeholder engagement plans have been developed.

☐ Yes   ☐ No   ☐ NA

A change response plan for managing the change has been developed and is comprised of:

- Key indicators of success

- Off track warning signs

- Details of actions to take when off track signs are observed

☐ Yes   ☐ No   ☐ NA

A plan to align relevant performance systems and structures to solutions and the new level of performance has been developed.

☐ Yes   ☐ No   ☐ NA

Solutions and the implementation plan have been validated with the process owner, project champion and relevant key stakeholders.

☐ Yes   ☐ No   ☐ NA

Project storyboard has been updated.

☐ Yes   ☐ No   ☐ NA

Lean Specific Project

Solutions for treating sources of waste were identified with the involvement of key process participants / operators.

☐ Yes   ☐ No   ☐ NA

Unintended consequences of implementing proposed solutions have been identified and a plan created for dealing with these.

☐ Yes   ☐ No   ☐ NA

A risk management plan has been put in place to deal with risks that affect the achievement of implementation project objectives.

☐ Yes   ☐ No   ☐ NA

A training plan for aligning skills to the requirements of the solution has been prepared.

☐ Yes   ☐ No   ☐ NA

Have developed a communications plan to support implementation.

☐ Yes   ☐ No   ☐ NA

Anticipated levels of commitment to proposed solutions have been analysed and stakeholder engagement plans have been developed.

☐ Yes   ☐ No   ☐ NA

A change response plan for managing the change has been developed and is comprised of:

- Key indicators of success

- Off track warning signs

- Details of actions to take when off track signs are observed

    ☐ Yes   ☐ No   ☐ NA

A plan to align relevant performance systems and structures to solutions and the new level of performance has been developed.

    ☐ Yes   ☐ No   ☐ NA

Solutions and the implementation plan have been validated with the process owner, project champion and relevant key stakeholders.

    ☐ Yes   ☐ No   ☐ NA

Project storyboard has been updated.

    ☐ Yes   ☐ No   ☐ NA

CONTROL Phase Checklist

Lean and Six Sigma Projects

The new process has been documented and institutionalised through relevant training.

☐ Yes   ☐ No   ☐ NA

Measures for monitoring performance of the process have been selected.

☐ Yes   ☐ No   ☐ NA

A performance monitoring plan that describes how performance will be monitored has been generated.

☐ Yes   ☐ No   ☐ NA

A statistical process control plan defining corrective action to take when specific triggers are observed has been put into effect.

☐ Yes   ☐ No   ☐ NA

The closure of the project can be formally recognised as a specific point in time.

☐ Yes   ☐ No   ☐ NA

The process owner has formally taken responsibility for the future performance of the process.

☐ Yes   ☐ No   ☐ NA

The project storyboard / poster has been updated.

☐ Yes   ☐ No   ☐ NA

The contribution of the team in the projects success has been formally celebrated.

☐ Yes   ☐ No   ☐ NA

The performance of the process has been monitored over time, and the goals of the project have been achieved.

☐ Yes   ☐ No   ☐ NA

_____

Wrap Up

Well folks, that's it.

I'll leave you with these thoughts and reminders.

Ask the tough questions during your projects, particularly those that relate to the business case. Remember, any business improvement initiative that does not deliver against business objectives *will* eventually be eliminated.

Never be afraid to drop a project, even midway through completion, if it is not going to bring value to the organisation.

There is no *one way* to complete a project. Stay focused on the outcome and only do what you need to do to achieve it.

I wish you good fortune, see you in my next book.

George Lee Sye

About the Author

George Lee Sye was born in 1959, he has found his niche as an author, influence and persuasion educator, and business improvement trainer and coach.

George founded Soarent Vision Pty Ltd in 2000 and has continually run that company as Managing Director.

He founded his first Professional Learning Hub in 2016, and then converted this into what is now the 9 Skills Factory professional development platform. He is the site's lead trainer and this is where he delivers the bulk of the business improvement (lean six sigma and leadership) education to the world.

George launched his podcast The George Experiment in 2018.

His breadth and depth of knowledge is drawn from a diverse range of experiences and life-long commitment to self education - from tradesman - to counter terrorism expert - to protecting the President of the United States of America; from working in horse stables - to Training Manager - to Hospital Administrator - to Company Owner.

Tens of thousands of people have personally experienced his philosophies in formal training courses and seminars, and connected with his incredible enthusiasm and energy for life through his work.

Since 2002 he has written 17 books, most of which are now distributed on Amazon and on iTunes in digital form.

George is also an avid motorcycle enthusiast with the ultimate part time job as an on track ride coach with the California Superbike School.

For more information about George and his work, visit his websites:

www.georgeleesye.com

www.9skillsfactory.com

www.thegeorgeexperiment.com

---------- END ----------

Lightning Source UK Ltd.
Milton Keynes UK
UKHW020638120422
401447UK00010B/1932

9 780648 968368